NAPOLEON BONAPARTE

Brian Williams

Designed by David Nash

Illustrators
Michael Lynn • Roger Payne
Bernard Robinson • Gareth Williams

Ray Rourke Publishing Company, Inc.
Windermere, Florida 32786

Published by Ray Rourke Publishing Company, Inc.,
Windermere, Florida 32786.
Copyright © 1979 Piper Books Ltd.
Copyright © 1981 Ray Rourke Publishing Company, Inc.

Library of Congress Cataloging in Publication Data

Williams, Brian.
  Napoléon Bonaparte.

  1. Napoléon I, Emperor of the French, 1769-1821—
Juvenile literature.   2. France—Kings and rulers—
Biography—Juvenile literature.   I. Lynn, Michael.
II. Title.
DC203.W533   1981   944.05'092'4   [B]   81-300
ISBN 0-86592-054-0   AACR1

NAPOLEON BONAPARTE

Out of the chaos of the French Revolution
rose a great leader — Napoleon Bonaparte. He
restored order to the troubled nation and
crowned himself Emperor. But his vanity was
not content with France; he must rule all
Europe. Napoleon's seemingly invincible
armies marched from one brilliant victory to
another, until, in 1815, his career was brought
to an abrupt end on the battlefield
of Waterloo.

4

The Young Corsican

In 1789 there was great excitement in France. People had lived too long under the bad government of their kings. The poor paid heavy taxes, while the rich nobles paid none. The middle classes could not change the laws as there was no legislature. So the people rose up, and demanded great changes. A new government was formed, dedicated to the ideals of Liberty, Equality and Brotherhood.

The spirit of unrest had spread to areas of French influence abroad. Napoleon Buonaparte was born in 1769 on the Mediterranean island of Corsica. His father, Carlo, was a poor nobleman. The year before, Corsica had become part of France.

Carlo Buonaparte sent his two eldest sons, Napoleon and Joseph, to a French military college. Napoleon worked hard but made few friends. In 1785 he became a second lieutenant in an artillery regiment. But his father died, and he had to return to Corsica to help his family. Napoleon offered his services to Pasquale Paoli, a Corsican leader. But Paoli thought the young French-trained officer was a "foreigner" and rejected him.

Napoleon supported the Revolution with enthusiasm. In Paris he went to radical clubs and made speeches against the nobles and the Church. He returned to Corsica in an attempt to persuade the Corsicans to join France and share in the Revolution. For a time he was listed as a deserter by his regiment.

However, Pasquale Paoli wanted no rivals and in June 1793 Napoleon and his family were forced to flee from the island. In France they changed their name from "Buonaparte" to "Bonaparte". From now on Napoleon was a Frenchman, and a soldier of the Revolution.

When the French Republic dissolved into bitter chaos, one man saved the day. Napoleon Bonaparte brought order back to France. Even when he made himself Emperor he always claimed to be fighting for the ideas of the Revolutuon.

The French Revolution put power into the hands of the masses. They had suffered so much under bad government that they turned on the nobles. Executions became a popular public spectacle. The guillotine was the official instrument of execution.

The Revolutionary Officer

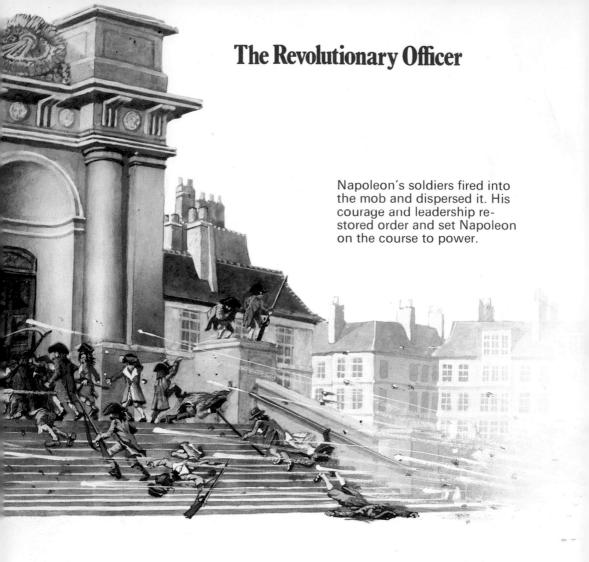

Napoleon's soldiers fired into the mob and dispersed it. His courage and leadership restored order and set Napoleon on the course to power.

France was in turmoil. The Convention, the revolutionary government, had executed the King and Queen for treason. Britain, Austria and Prussia had declared war on the new Republic. Volunteers flocked to defend the Revolution, but they were hard pressed. Power passed to three men – Danton, Marat, and Robespierre. Their reign was known as the Reign of Terror. Thousands perished on the guillotine.

Napoleon was with his regiment in the south. Royalists and British forces had captured the port of Toulon. Napoleon led his gunners to storm the city. The victory earned him the chance of quick promotion.

But the people were sick of the Reign of Terror. Marat was murdered, and Danton and Robespierre were guillotined. Napoleon himself was imprisoned. He was freed only because France needed soldiers to drive out the invaders – and to quell unrest at home.

In Paris angry mobs took to the streets. The Convention itself was under attack. Its leader, Barras, recalled Napoleon. In October, 1795, Napoleon brought his cannon into the city, barred the streets and scattered the mob with salvoes of grapeshot. Barras became head of a new government, the Directory. He pointed out Napoleon to his colleagues. "Advance this man," he said, "or he will advance himself without you".

Promotion followed quickly. Napoleon succeeded Barras in command of the Army of the Interior. He courted and married a beautiful widow, Josephine de Beauharnais (whose husband had been one of the thousands of nobles executed by guillotine during the Terror). Then he was given a new command – the French Army of Italy.

It was not a popular appointment. "You are too young", grumbled an old general. "In a year", replied Napoleon, "I shall either be old or dead".

Italy and Egypt

It was his greatest challenge yet. The army was ill-equipped and untrained. Austria controlled most of the small Italian kingdoms, and Napoleon realized that he would need new tactics to beat the disciplined Austrian troops. So he trained his army to march swiftly and to live off the land. He gathered about him dashing young officers, such as the brilliant cavalry leader Joachim Murat. Yet he always made time to listen to the advice – and the grumbles – of the ordinary soldier. His men soon knew him fondly as the "Little Corporal".

The slow-moving Austrian armies were baffled by the speed of the French. The Austrian generals foolishly divided their forces. Napoleon routed them. In one battle, 6000 Austrians surrendered to only 500 French troops! In little over a year Napoleon was master of Italy.

In April 1797 the defeated Austrians made peace on Napoleon's terms. He returned to France a national hero. The government was alarmed. Would success make Napoleon too ambitious? So they were pleased when he suggested an expedition to Egypt – a first step in a plan to attack the British empire in India. "Europe is but a molehill; all the great glories have come from Asia," Napoleon declared.

In May 1798 a French fleet of 27 warships and 400 transports set sail. Malta was easily captured and an army of 40,000 landed in Egypt. Napoleon took with him scientists, archeologists, and artists to study the Land of the Pharaohs.

The rulers of Egypt were the fierce Mamelukes. Before the Battle of the Pyramids in July 1798 Napoleon told his troops: "Soldiers, forty centuries look down on you!" The well-drilled French formed squares to fight off the wild rushes of the Mameluke horsemen. Musket volleys did the rest.

After the French victory, Napoleon marched into Cairo. He visited the Great Pyramid, while his scientists eagerly packed up mummies, sculptures, and other relics for shipment to Paris.

The Rosetta Stone, found by Napoleon's soldiers in Egypt, gave scholars the key to deciphering Egyptian hieroglyphics.

But almost immediately after this triumph came disaster. The French fleet was surprised by the British admiral, Horatio Nelson. The British ships sailed boldly into the shallow harbor; only two French vessels managed to escape. Napoleon's dream of conquering India was ended. He and his army were marooned in Egypt.

Mameluke prisoners and their French captors after the Battle of the Pyramids.

The Dictator

Napoleon swiftly reorganized the government of Egypt on European lines. Leaving a French general to rule the country, he set off overland to attack Syria. He hoped to fight his way home through the Turkish Empire. But he got no farther than Acre. There the Turks and a small British force held fast. After a siege lasting 60 days, and with disease ravaging his army, Napoleon was forced to retreat.

Meanwhile, Austria was back in the war and the French were losing ground in Italy. News of defeats caused discontent at home. Friends of Napoleon urged him to return without delay and seize power.

He boarded a frigate secretly and sailed for France. He managed to avoid the British men-of-war that were searching the Mediterranean for him. In October 1799 he arrived in Paris. Backed by his guards, he marched boldly into the legislature and dismissed the members. The Directory collapsed, and a new government, the Consulate, replaced it.

Three Consuls were named to rule France: Sieyès, Ducos, and Bonaparte. In fact, Napoleon was sole ruler. He was named First Consul. The revolutionary Republic was no more. At the age of 30 Napoleon was a dictator.

The First Consul threw himself into the task of government with enormous energy. He took personal responsibility for appointing officials and army commanders. He made many important reforms: modernizing local government, reforming the old-

fashioned tax laws, encouraging the building of new roads, bridges, and canals. He set up the Bank of France, and created a new honor for outstanding people – the Legion of Honor. He also made a treaty with the Pope, ending the split with the Roman Catholic Church which the Revolution had brought about.

These changes gave France a firm government after the confusion of the Revolution. Napoleon's new laws – the Napoleonic Code – are still the basis of French law today.

The army remained Napoleon's first concern. Every Frenchman had to serve as a soldier; but promotion was open to all, rich or poor. Napoleon founded military academies to train the sons of ordinary families as officers.

Napoleon wrote personal letters to the Emperor of Austria and the King of England. They did not reply. Europe's kings wanted nothing to do with the "upstart" ruler of France. Only by victory on the battlefield could the war be won.

The new First Consul is installed.

13

The General

Crossing the St Bernard Pass. The soldiers embedded their cannon in split tree trunks, to protect them from damage.

In the spring of 1800 Napoleon led his army across the Alps into Italy to fight the Austrians again. Snow still lay deep in the mountains. The soldiers struggled over the St. Bernard Pass, dragging their cannon on sledges.

Like Hannibal centuries before, the French took the enemy by surprise. The Austrians suffered defeat after defeat, the heaviest at the Battle of Marengo on June 14th, 1800. The Austrian army of 30,000 outnumbered the French by 8000 men, and at first Napoleon seemed to be doomed to defeat. Then he threw in his reserve troops, rode along the lines to rally the French infantry, and led the attack which won the day.

In July 1800 he returned to Paris. Cheering crowds flocked to the Tuileries, the former royal palace where Napoleon now lived. Amid the rejoicing at his triumph, he narrowly escaped death. A bomb exploded as he drove through the streets on his way to the opera. The explosion came just half a minute after his carriage had passed. Twenty people were killed, but Napoleon was unhurt.

When, in 1801, Austria once more

made peace, only Britain remained at war with France. Napoleon assembled an invasion fleet of barges at Boulogne and made plans to land in England and capture London. However, he knew that an invasion could never succeed while the British fleet patrolled the English Channel. The invasion was postponed and in 1802 Britain too made peace.

Napoleon was now voted Consul for life. Many British visitors traveled to France, eager to see the changes brought about by the Revolution. To their surprise, they found Napoleon ruling very much like a king. And instead of calling one another Citizen (as they had in the days of "Equality"), the French people had gone back to the old titles Monsieur and Madame.

Right: A soldier of the Consular Guard. This regiment, nicknamed "The Invincibles", was Napoleon's personal escort and bodyguard. Its members served with courage in every one of Napoleon's campaigns. When Napoleon became Emperor, the Consular Guard became the Imperial Guard. Officers and men carried sabers and pistols, and the ordinary soldiers also carried carbines and bayonets.

The Emperor

The fragile peace was short-lived. Britain feared that Napoleon planned to conquer the whole of Europe and then seize her overseas empire. In 1803 the war began again.

Britain sent money to Austria and Russia to help raise new armies against Napoleon. The British also plotted with French royalists to assassinate him. But every plot was discovered and the plotters were executed. Napoleon dealt harshly with all who opposed him.

From dictator to monarch was only a short step, and in 1804 Napoleon had himself elected Emperor of the French. His heirs (as yet he had no children) were to succeed him – thus founding a new royal family. His brothers were made princes and old titles were revived as gifts for his favorite commanders. Seventeen generals were made Marshals of the Empire, among them Murat, Massena, Bernadotte, Soult and Ney.

Supporters of the old Republic looked on indignantly, but could do nothing. Even nobles were returning from exile to join the new French court. But the soldiers cheered their Emperor and the Pope himself came to Paris for Napoleon's coronation.

The Grand Army of the Empire prepared to fight again. Its ranks now included recruits from all over Europe. At its heart stood the Imperial Guards, always held in reserve until the crucial moment of battle.

Even as he planned the downfall of the Austrians and Russians, Napoleon looked longingly across the English Channel. Another invasion fleet had

assembled and an army of 160,000 men was camped along the coasts of France and Holland. Napoleon was confident of victory – if only his army could reach England. He ordered the French fleet to decoy the British ships away long enough for the invasion barges to slip across the Channel.

Napoleon's plan depended on a victory at sea. But when news came, it was of a naval disaster. The British had won the Battle of Trafalgar (October 21, 1805). Nelson was dead. But of 33 French and Spanish ships, only 15 had escaped.

Ironically, the Grand Army had already packed its tents before the first guns were fired at Trafalgar. For Napoleon could no longer ignore the Austrian and Russian armies at his back. He turned away from Britain and marched east.

The pomp and splendor of the Imperial coronation. Napoleon took the crown and placed it on his own head. Then he crowned Josephine as Empress. Right: Napoleon's second Empress, Marie-Louise, whom he married in 1810.

Master of Europe

Napoleon dreamed of building a European empire greater than the empires of Charlemagne or of Rome, with Paris for its capital.

He had already redrawn the map of Europe. He had abolished age-old frontiers and set up small kingdoms and republics under French control. The victories of the Grand Army would weld Europe into one glorious French Empire.

The Austrians were defeated at Ulm, shortly before news of Trafalgar reached Napoleon. Two months later he won his most brilliant victory, at Austerlitz.

Austerlitz (now called Slavkov u Brna) is a village in present-day Czechoslovakia. The French had already captured Vienna and the combined Austrian-Russian army, 87,000 strong had retreated to hold the high ground. Napoleon's army of 73,000 advanced to attack them.

Napoleon after his triumph at Austerlitz.

Napoleon left his right flank weak, tempting the enemy to attack it. The enemy fell for the ruse. They moved troops from the center of their line and left the high ground.

The French right held. At once Marshal Soult and 20,000 French infantry stormed up the hill to break through the enemy center. Napoleon rushed his guns after the infantry and from the high ground the French cannon poured a cruel fire onto the mass of enemy troops caught in the valley below.

The allied army was split and fled in disorder. Austria immediately made peace. In 1806 Napoleon beat the Prussians at Jena and captured Berlin. In 1807, after bloody battles at Eylau and Friedland, he forced Russia out of the war. He met the Russian Czar on a raft in the middle of the River Niemen to sign the Treaty of Tilsit. This was the peak of Napoleon's power.

Kingdom of Sweden

Denmark and Norway

Russian Empire

Prussia

United Kingdom

Grand Duchy of Warsaw

Confederation of the Rhine

French Empire

Austrian Empire

Switzerland   Italy

Illyrian Province

Ottoman Empire

Portugal

Spain

Corsica   Naples

Sardinia

Sicily

French Empire

Allied with Napoleon

Controlled by Napoleon

The Tide Turns

But all was not well with the Empire. Britain was an implacable enemy, safe behind a powerful navy. Unable to conquer Britain, Napoleon tried to strangle its trade. But the trade blockade was very difficult to enforce. Even Napoleon's brother Louis, King of Holland, seemed to ignore it. Napoleon, furious, forced Louis to give up his throne.

The Imperial court loved splendid parties and balls. But the Empire was already doomed; its army was on the run in the Peninsula.

And Britain still had allies. One of them was Portugal. To plug this gap in his blockade, Napoleon sent an army through Spain to seize the Portuguese capital, Lisbon. Britain sent troops to help Portugal. When Spain protested at the invasion, Napoleon forced the King of Spain to abdicate and put his own brother Joseph on the throne. Spanish pride was insulted and the people rose in revolt. The Peninsular War had begun.

In the autumn of 1808 a new general, Arthur Wellesley (later Duke of Wellington), landed in Portugal to lead the British army. The fighting was hard and the French began to lose ground to the new British commander.

Napoleon had to leave the Spanish war to his generals, for in 1809 Austria again declared war. He captured Vienna yet again and defeated the Austrians at the Battle of Wagram.

Napoleon still had no son. So he divorced Josephine, and for his new Empress chose Marie-Louise, daughter of the Austrian Emperor. She arrived in Paris in 1810 to find her rooms in the Tuileries decorated to match exactly her old home in Vienna.

Right: French forces retreating after defeats in the Peninsular War.

In 1811 the Empress gave birth to a son. Napoleon was delighted and proclaimed the baby King of Rome. Now that he had an heir, he felt more confident.

Yet the war in Spain dragged on. Napoleon complained bitterly that his generals could do nothing without him. But he was far away in Paris, and faced with another war, against Russia. For Czar Alexander of Russia had refused to stop trading with Britain, despite all Napoleon's threats. "In five years," the Emperor raged, "I shall be master of the world. I shall break Russia in pieces."

The Retreat from Moscow

In the summer of 1812 the Grand Army gathered beside the Niemen river in Lithuania. As Napoleon rode to review his troops, his horse stumbled and he almost fell. Was this a bad omen for the future?

The invasion army was the largest Europe had ever seen – 450,000 men. Yet many of Napoleon's advisers were afraid. Russia was too large, its population too great. Talleyrand, his foreign minister, begged the Emperor to turn back. Napoleon refused; he believed he was following the star of his destiny.

The French advanced into Russia. But instead of fighting, the Russians retreated, burning villages and crops

as they went. Not until September did the Grand Army come within sight of Moscow. At last there was a full-scale battle, at Borodino. Both sides suffered heavy losses, and neither had a clear victory.

After Borodino, the Russians fell back in good order, evacuating Moscow. The eager French soldiers found the city deserted. There was hardly any food and many buildings had been set on fire. Napoleon waited for the Czar to surrender. No word came and in October the first snow fell.

With no warm winter clothing, and with their supplies running out, the French had no choice but to retreat. The retreat became a fight for survival. Men killed their horses for food and froze to death as they sat around their dying camp fires. Day

The retreating army was harassed by raiding parties of Russia's fiercest mounted warriors – the Cossacks.

and night, Russian Cossacks attacked the starving men. Each day the army grew smaller. As many as 250,000 men died, and thousands more were taken prisoner.

News of this disaster caused dismay in Paris. There were rumors that Napoleon himself was dead. Napoleon decided he must abandon the army and return home as quickly as possible.

He arrived as the year drew to a close. France rejoiced to see him alive. "Only the Russian winter defeated me," he explained, "not the Russian army." And he began raising fresh regiments.

As he did so the pitiful survivors of the Grand Army limped home. Fewer than 40,000 fighting men came back across the Niemen.

Allied troops in the streets of occupied Paris. Right: Napoleon's farewell to the loyal Imperial Guard.

The Hundred Days

France was now under attack from all sides. The allies were determined to end the French Empire. The emperors of Austria, Russia, and Prussia led their armies against Napoleon. Wellington, victorious in the Peninsula, crossed the Pyrenees into France. In

met in secret with Louis, the brother of the executed King, and agreed that Louis should become King after Napoleon's fall. Paris surrendered without a fight. Napoleon heard the news at Fontainebleau. Persuaded by his marshals that the war was lost, he abdicated. The allies agreed to let him live in exile on the Mediterranean island of Elba.

On Elba he soon recovered his spirits and set about "improving" his tiny realm. But he had little money and grieved because his wife and son had been taken to Austria.

The new King, known to his subjects as "Louis the Pig" because he was so fat, was unpopular almost immediately. It was as if the Republic and Empire had never existed. Many royalist exiles returned to reclaim their lands. But the French people had no wish to go back to the bad old days.

Napoleon sailed secretly from Elba and landed near Cannes. He had a tiny army – 500 guards, 200 dragoons, and 100 lancers without horses – yet within days its number had swelled to thousands. Soldiers sent to arrest him rushed to greet him, crying "Long live the Emperor!" Marshal Ney, who had promised to bring Napoleon back to Paris "like a wild beast in a cage" begged forgiveness and joined him.

As he neared Paris, Napoleon sent out a stream of orders. The army was to prepare for war. The King's government was abolished, and Louis slipped away to Holland. Back in the Tuileries, Napoleon announced that he had returned to save the Revolution. "The people called; I came", he declared, as the last act of his reign, known to history as the Hundred Days, began.

October 1813 the French were defeated at Leipzig, in the Battle of the Nations. The allies marched on Paris.

Napoleon fought a brilliant defensive campaign. But his troops were mostly tired veterans and untrained boys. Outnumbered and exhausted, the French army no longer had the stomach for war.

The end came swiftly. Talleyrand

Waterloo

Napoleon knew that his hastily recruited army could not match the combined might of the allies. He must strike quickly, split his enemies, and by swift victories hope to force a peace treaty.

The French army invaded Belgium and on June 16 Napoleon beat the Prussians at Ligny. He ordered Marshal Grouchy to pursue the Prussian army and prevent it joining forces with Wellington's army. Napoleon, with 72,000 men, advanced to meet Wellington at Waterloo, a village 9 miles (15 km.) south of Brussels.

Wellington had an army of 68,000 – British, Dutch, Belgians and Germans. He sent a message to the Prussian Field Marshal, Blucher, urging him to bring his army to Waterloo. Having received Blucher's promise, Wellington prepared to do battle.

Waterloo; a Highland
regiment drives off
French cavalry.

The Battle of Waterloo was fought on June 18, 1815. Napoleon waited until noon before attacking, for the ground was wet after overnight rain. This delay proved fatal. Time after time the French failed to break through the British lines. But by 6 o'clock they had captured a key position, the farmhouse of La Haye Sainte, and were poised for victory.

The arrival of Blucher swung the battle away from Napoleon. The Prussian army of 42,000, having eluded Grouchy's pursuit, swept in to attack the French flank. In a last desperate bid to break Wellington's infantry, Napoleon sent in his Imperial Guards. But the gallant veterans crumbled before the point-blank fire of the British. The French attack wavered, and became a retreat. Harried by the Prussians, the French army fled in confusion.

Napoleon drove away in a carriage. He knew that all was lost. Four days later he abdicated a second time. He tried to take ship for America but was stopped by the British. On board the warship Bellerophon anchored in Plymouth Sound, Napoleon's appearance on deck was greeted by cheers from sailors on other ships.

The British sent him into exile once more, this time to the lonely island of St. Helena in the South Atlantic. There Napoleon spent his last few years, a sick man. In 1821 he died. He was buried on St. Helena; but in 1840 his remains were brought back to Paris and reburied in Les Invalides, the hostel for wounded soldiers built by King Louis XIV. The exiled Emperor had come home.

Napoleon sails away to his final exile on St. Helena.

Important Dates

1769	Napoleon born on August 15 at Ajaccio, Corsica	**1804**	Napoleon is crowned Emperor
1785	Commissioned in La Fère regiment	**1805**	Battles of Trafalgar and Austerlitz France tries to strangle Britain's trade
1789	Fall of the Bastille		
1792	France at war with Austria and Prussia Abolition of the monarchy by the Convention	**1806**	Battles of Jena and Auerstädt
		1807	Peace of Tilsit France invades Portugal
1793	Execution of King Louis XVI The Reign of Terror Napoleon recaptures Toulon	**1808**	Peninsular War begins
		1810	Napoleon marries Marie-Louise of Austria
1795	The Directory replaces the Convention	**1812**	The Russian campaign
1796	Napoleon marries Josephine Takes command of the Army of Italy	**1813**	Battle of Leipzig
		1814	Allied invasion of France Abdication of Napoleon Exile to Elba
1798	Napoleon in Egypt		
1799	Napoleon becomes First Consul	**1815**	Napoleon's return to France The Battle of Waterloo Exile to St. Helena
1800	Battle of Marengo		
1802	Peace of Amiens	**1821**	Death of Napoleon on May 5

POSTSCRIPT

Napoleon's son, although known as Napoleon II, in fact never became Emperor. He remained at the Austrian court until his death in 1832. Napoleon's nephew, Louis Napoleon (the son of Louis Bonaparte, King of Holland), was Emperor of France from 1852 to 1870 as Napoleon III. Curiously, Napoleon III's son, the Prince Imperial, joined the British army after his father's exile and was killed in 1879 while fighting the Zulus in South Africa.